KITCHENER PUBLIC LIBRARY

mscom
787
.871
66
Black
M

39098081019613

Turn blue

PLAY IT LIKE IT IS GUITAR

WITH TABLATURE

NOTE-FOR-NOTE TRANSCRIPTIONS

THE BLACK
TURN BLUE

Music transcriptions by Pete Billmann, Jeff Jacobson, Matt Scharfglass and David Stocker

ISBN 978-1-4803-9511-4

 cherry lane
music company

 EXCLUSIVELY DISTRIBUTED BY
HAL•LEONARD® CORPORATION
7777 W. BLUEMOUND RD. P.O. BOX 13819 MILWAUKEE, WI 53213

In Australia Contact:
Hal Leonard Australia Pty. Ltd.
4 Lentara Court
Cheltenham, Victoria, 3192 Australia
Email: ausadmin@halleonard.com.au

For all works contained herein:
Unauthorized copying, arranging, adapting, recording, Internet posting, publ
or other distribution of the printed music in this publication is an infringeme
Infringers are liable under the law.

D0814232

Visit Hal Leonard Online at
www.halleonard.com

Weight of Love

Words and Music by Dan Auerbach, Patrick Carney and Brian Burton

Intro
Moderately slow ♩ = 76

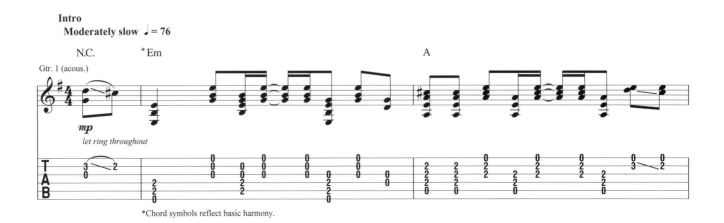

*Chord symbols reflect basic harmony.

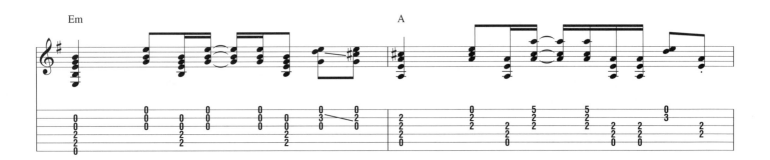

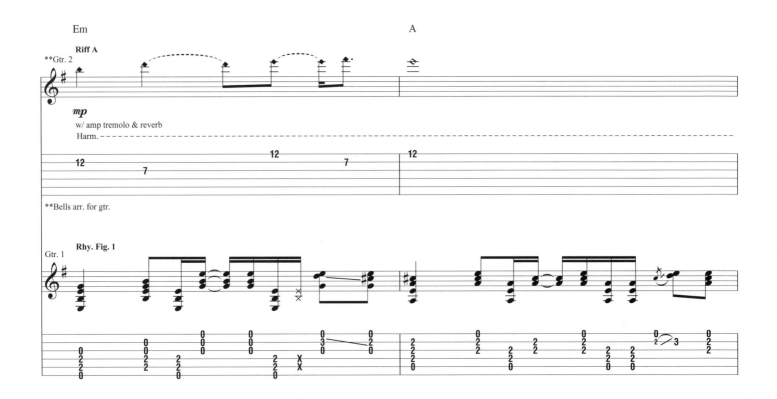

Copyright © 2014 McMoore McLesst Publishing (BMI) and Sweet Science (ASCAP)
All Rights on behalf of McMoore McLesst Publishing in the world excluding Australia and New Zealand Administered by Wixen Music Publishing, Inc.
All Rights on behalf of McMoore McLesst Publishing in Australia and New Zealand Administered by GaGa Music
All Rights Reserved   Used by Permission

3

Guitar Solo

Gtr. 1: w/ Rhy. Fig. 1 (3 times)
Gtr. 3: w/ Riff B (1 1/2 times)

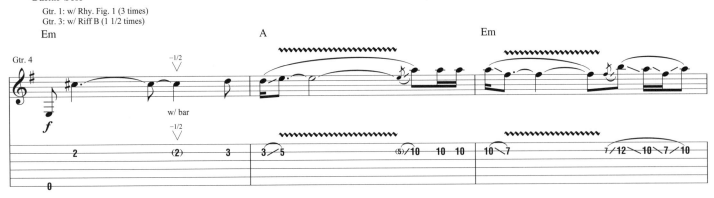

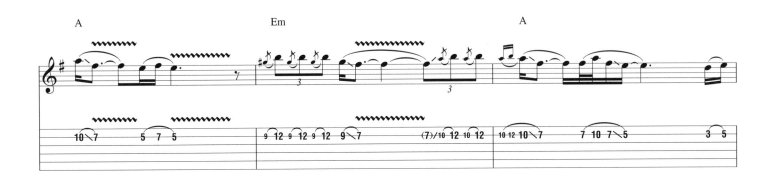

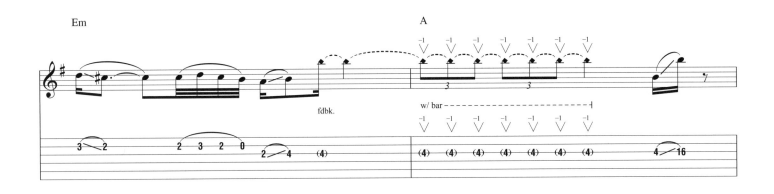

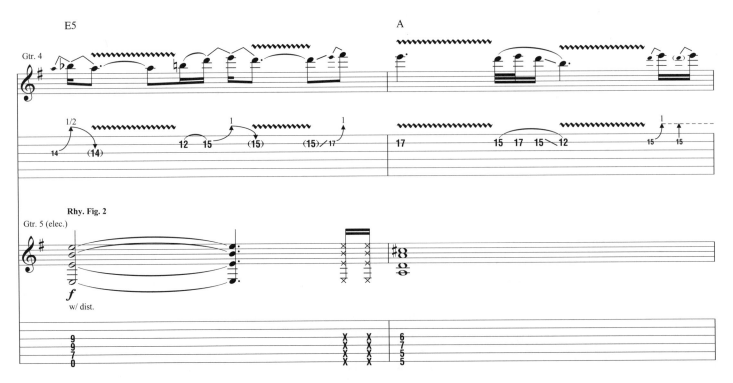

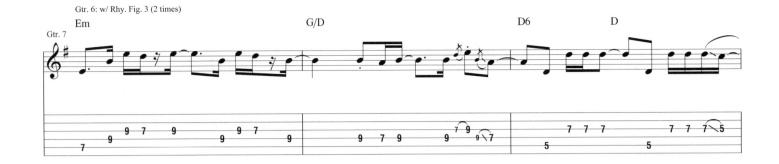

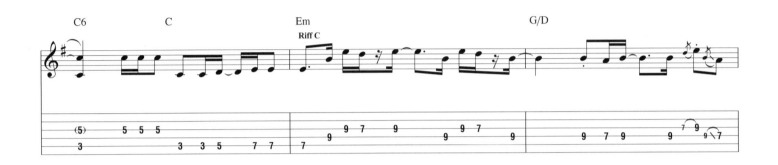

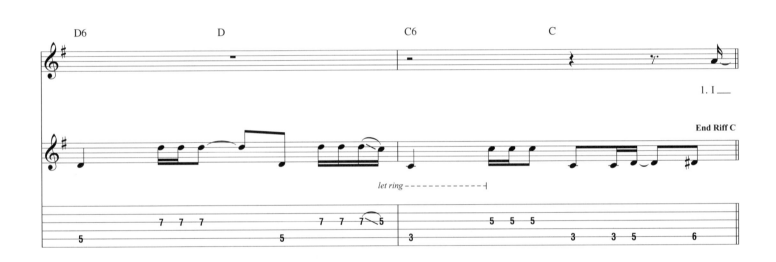

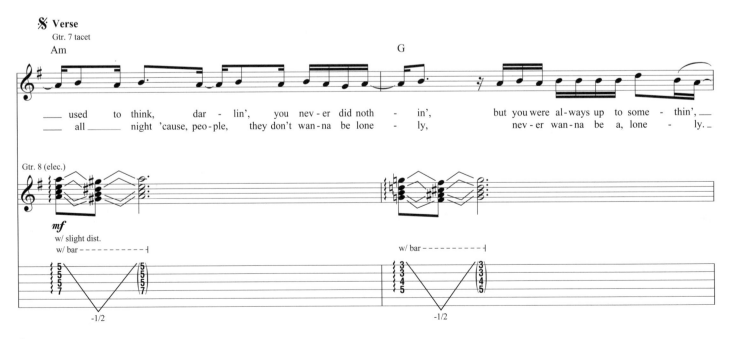

Interlude

Gtr. 1: w/ Rhy. Fig. 1
Gtr. 2: w/ Riff A
Gtr. 3: w/ Riff B (1st 4 meas.)
Gtrs. 8 & 9 tacet

Guitar Solo

Gtr. 1: w/ Rhy. Fig. 1 (2 times)
Gtr. 3: w/ Riff B (last 4 meas.)

Gtr. 3: w/ Riff B (1st 4 meas.)
Gtr. 5: w/ Rhy. Fig. 2

Interlude

Gtrs. 1 & 3: w/ Rhy. Fill 1
Gtr. 6: w/ Rhy. Fig. 3
Gtr. 7: w/ Riff C

Gtr. 4 tacet

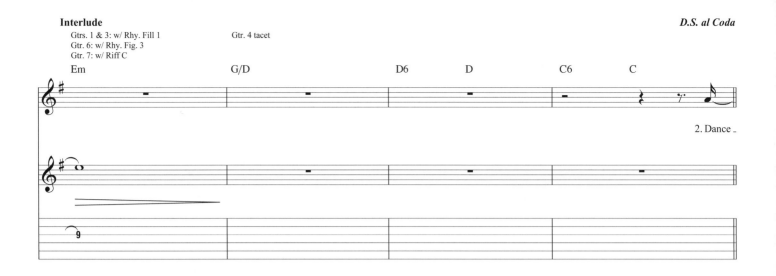

2. Dance

Coda

Gtr. 8: w/ Rhy. Fig. 4 (last meas.)

Interlude

Gtr. 8: w/ Rhy. Fig. 4 (3 times)
Gtr. 9: w/ Riff D (12 times)

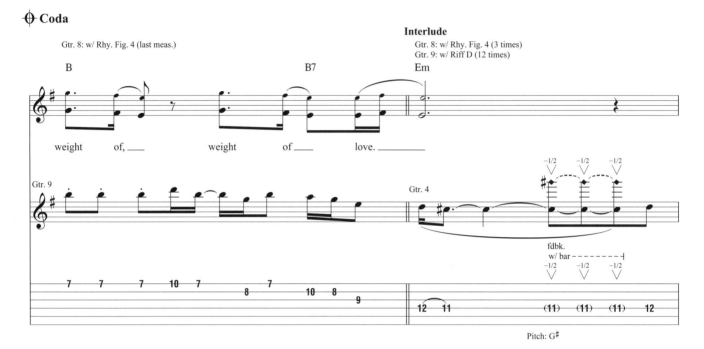

weight of, ___ weight of ___ love. ___

Gtr. 9

Gtr. 4

fdbk.
w/ bar

Pitch: G♯

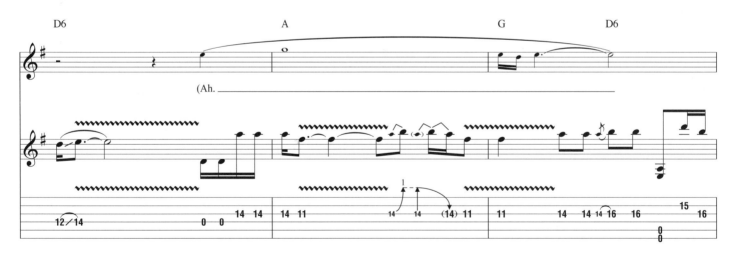

(Ah. ___

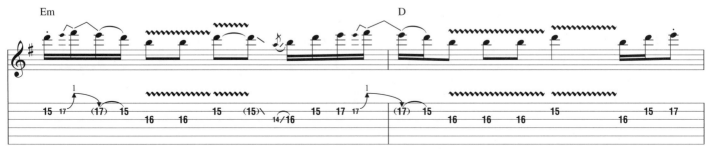

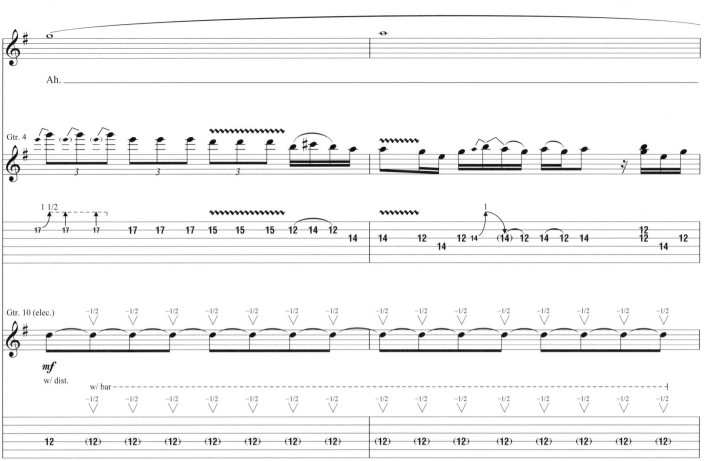

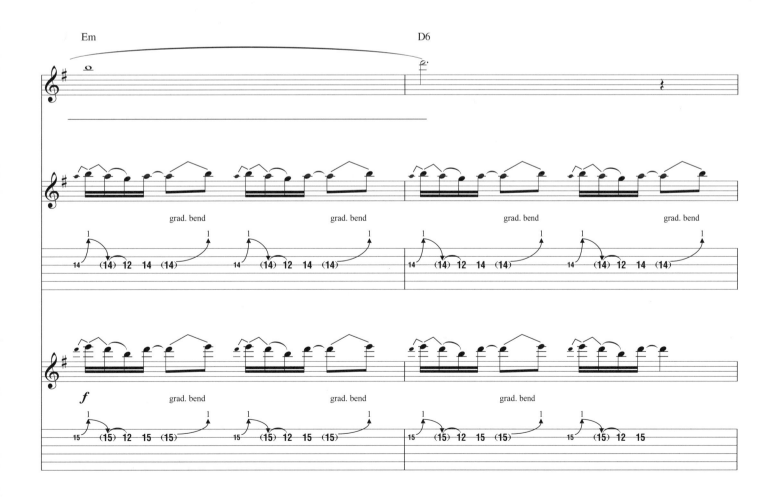

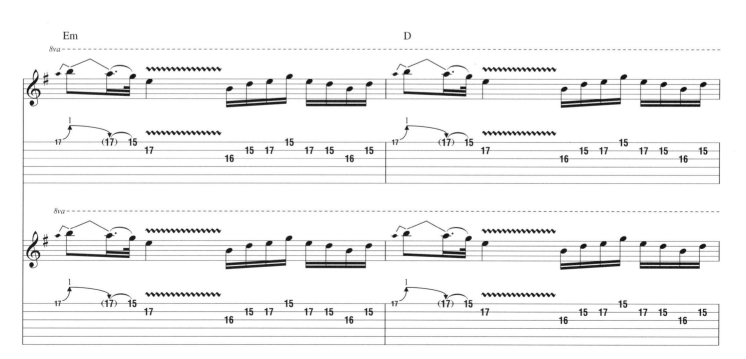

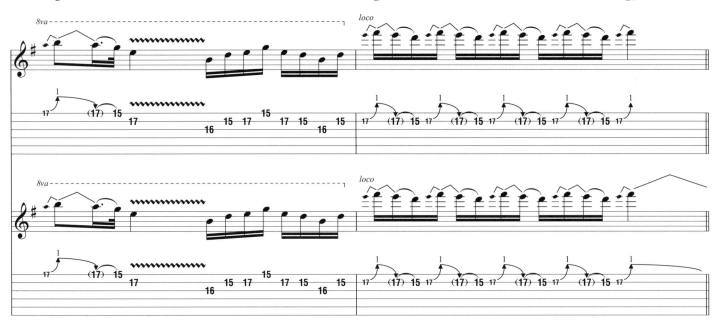

Interlude

In Time

Words and Music by Dan Auerbach, Patrick Carney and Brian Burton

Copyright © 2014 McMoore McLesst Publishing (BMI) and Sweet Science (ASCAP)
All Rights on behalf of McMoore McLesst Publishing in the world excluding Australia and New Zealand Administered by Wixen Music Publishing, Inc.
All Rights on behalf of McMoore McLesst Publishing in Australia and New Zealand Administered by GaGa Music
All Rights Reserved   Used by Permission

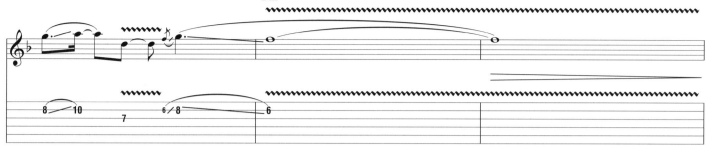

2nd & 3rd times, Gtr. 4: w/ Rhy. Fill 1

Dm

Gtr. 2 tacet

Gtr. 3 (12-str. elec.)

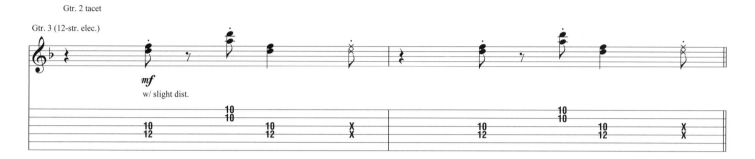

mf

w/ slight dist.

Verse

Dm

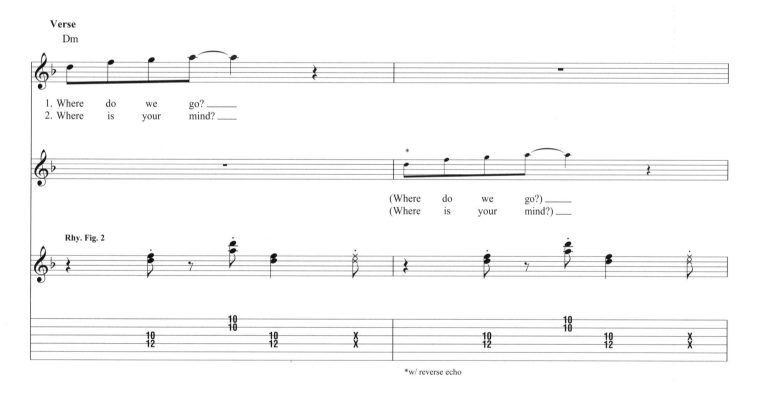

1. Where   do   we   go? _____
2. Where   is   your   mind? _____

(Where   do   we   go?) _____
(Where   is   your   mind?) _____

Rhy. Fig. 2

*w/ reverse echo

Am   Gm

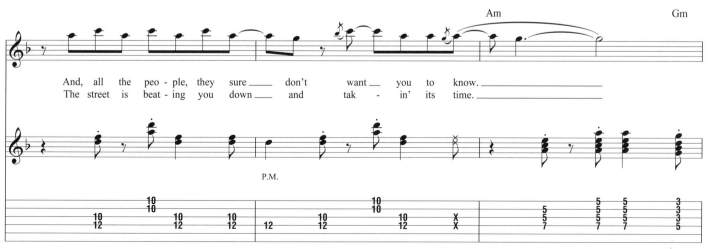

And, all the peo - ple, they sure ____ don't ____ want ____ you to know. ____
The street is beat - ing you down ____ and ____ tak - in' its time. ____

P.M.

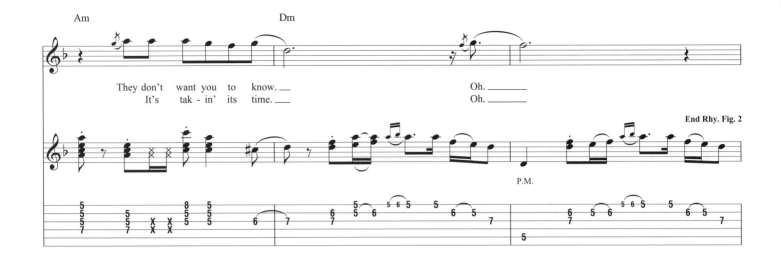

They don't want you to know. __ Oh. _____
It's tak - in' its time. __ Oh. _____

Gtr. 3: w/ Rhy. Fig. 2   2nd time, Bkgd. Voc.: w/ Voc. Fig. 2

Liv - in' in chains, __ thoughts __ re - ar - ranged. __   You got a wor - ried mind _____ all __ of the time. __
No - where to run. __   I told you to get ____ but you were hav - in' your fun. __

_____   Now tell me I'm ly - in'. Oh. ____   And
_____   Now you're un - der the gun. Oh. ____

Pre-Chorus

I got a thing I real - ly can't say. _____ Oh, __ oh, oh, __ oh.

Gtr. 3

Voc. Fig. 2

(No - where to run.) __

*w/ reverse echo

You got a wor - ried __ mind,   I got a wor - ried __ heart.   You don't know what to __ do,

I don't know where to __ start.   We let this get us __ down   or get up off the __ ground. __

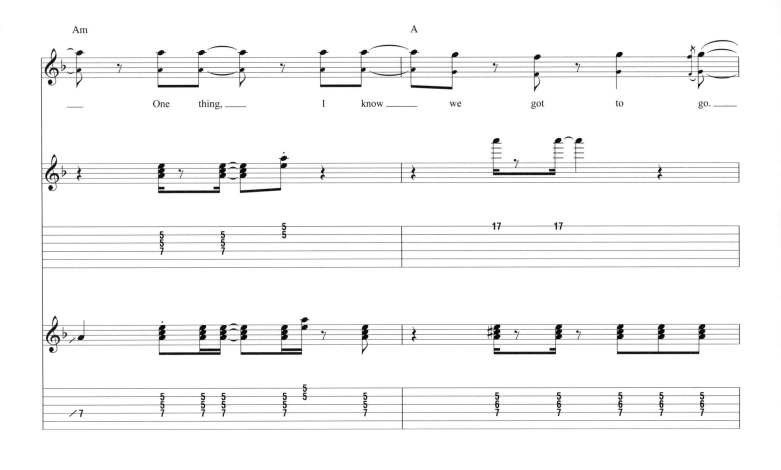

One thing, ____ I know ____ we got to go. ____

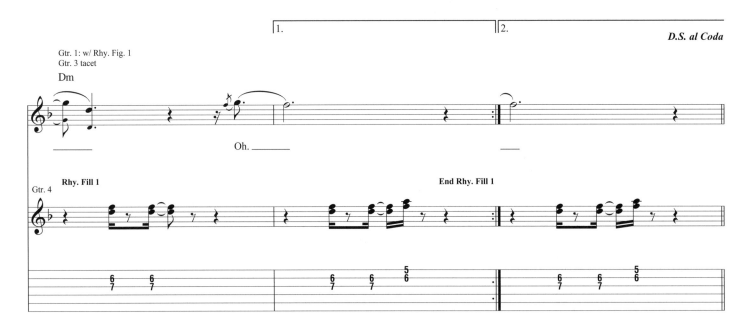

1.

2.

D.S. al Coda

Gtr. 1: w/ Rhy. Fig. 1
Gtr. 3 tacet

Dm

Oh. ____

Rhy. Fill 1
Gtr. 4   End Rhy. Fill 1

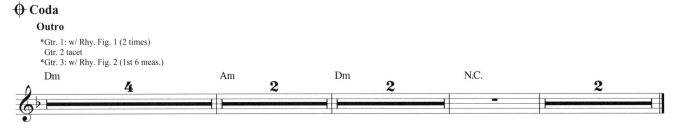

⊕ **Coda**

Outro

*Gtr. 1: w/ Rhy. Fig. 1 (2 times)
Gtr. 2 tacet
*Gtr. 3: w/ Rhy. Fig. 2 (1st 6 meas.)

Dm   Am   Dm   N.C.

4   **2**   **2**   **2**

*Gradually fade out.

Turn Blue

Words and Music by Dan Auerbach, Patrick Carney and Brian Burton

Copyright © 2014 McMoore McLesst Publishing (BMI) and Sweet Science (ASCAP)
All Rights on behalf of McMoore McLesst Publishing in the world excluding Australia and New Zealand Administered by Wixen Music Publishing, Inc.
All Rights on behalf of McMoore McLesst Publishing in Australia and New Zealand Administered by GaGa Music
All Rights Reserved   Used by Permission

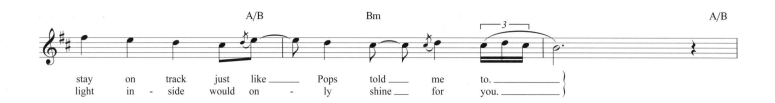

stay on track just like ____ Pops told ____ me to. ____
light in - side would on - ly shine ____ for you. ____

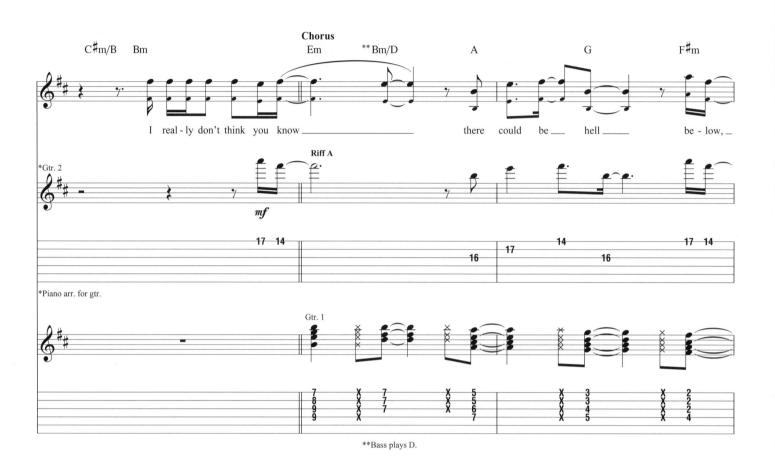

Chorus

I real - ly don't think you know ____ there could be ____ hell ____ be - low,

*Gtr. 2

*Piano arr. for gtr.

**Bass plays D.

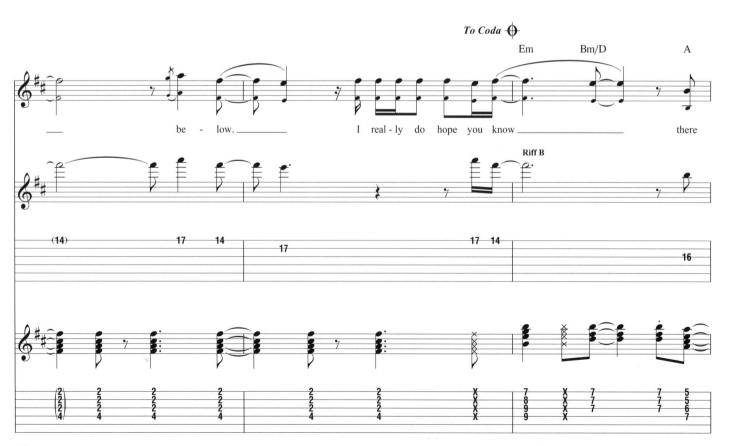

To Coda ⊕

____ be - low. ____ I real - ly do hope you know ____ there

Riff B

could be hell, _____ be-low, _____ be - low. _____

End Riff B

Interlude

Gtr. 2 tacet

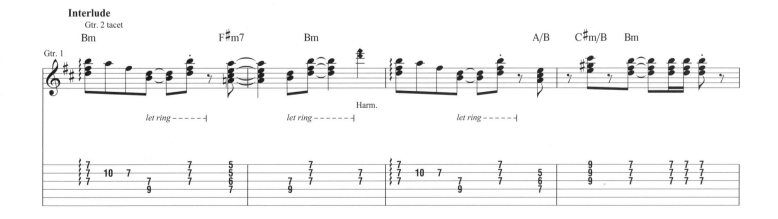

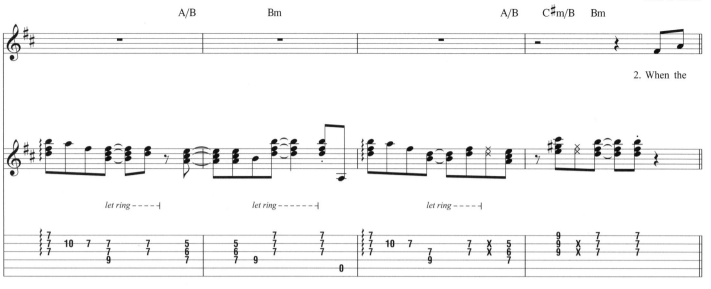

2. When the

⊕ Coda

there could be ___ hell, ___ be - low, ___ be - low. ___

I real - ly don't think you know ___ there could be ___ hell ___ be - low, ___

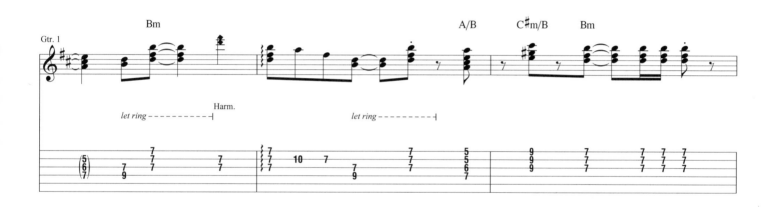

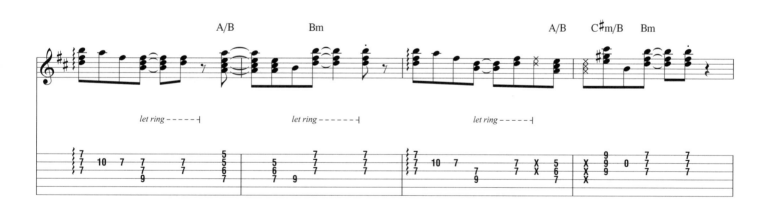

Fever

Words and Music by Dan Auerbach, Patrick Carney and Brian Burton

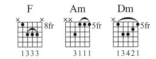

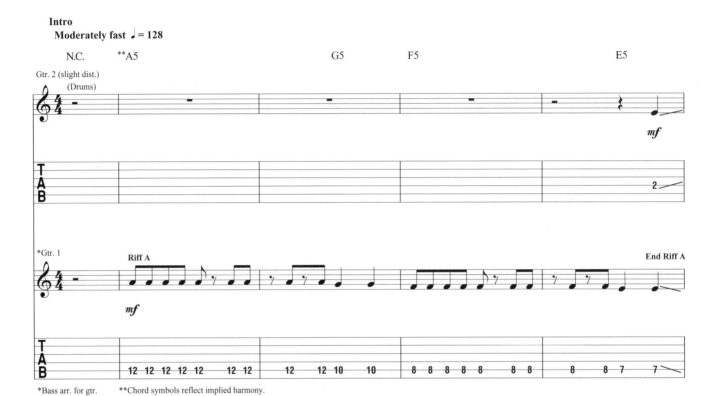

*Bass arr. for gtr.   **Chord symbols reflect implied harmony.

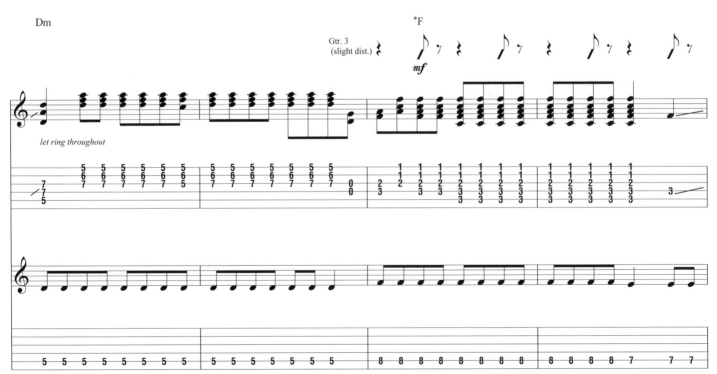

*See top of page for chord symbols pertaining to rhythm slashes.

Copyright © 2014 McMoore McLesst Publishing (BMI) and Sweet Science (ASCAP)
All Rights on behalf of McMoore McLesst Publishing in the world excluding Australia and New Zealand Administered by Wixen Music Publishing, Inc.
All Rights on behalf of McMoore McLesst Publishing in Australia and New Zealand Administered by GaGa Music
All Rights Reserved   Used by Permission

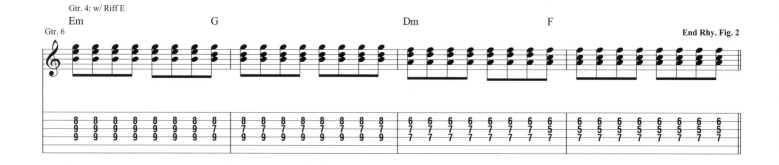

Gtr. 4: w/ Riff E

Gtr. 6

Em   G   Dm   F   **End Rhy. Fig. 2**

Bridge

Gtr. 4: w/ Riff E (2 times)
Gtr. 6: w/ Rhy. Fig. 2

Am   C/G   Am   C/G

Now, if the cold pale light in your eyes _____ reach - es those hor - i -

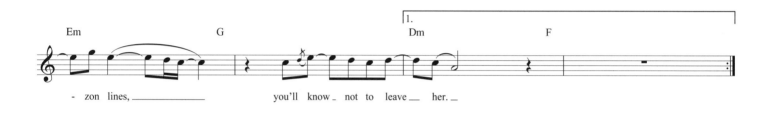

Em   G   1.   Dm   F

- zon lines, _____ you'll know _ not to leave _ her. _

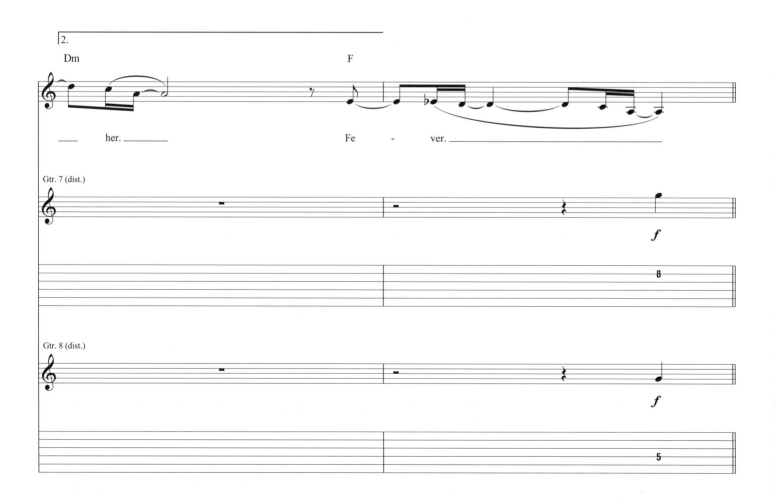

2.

Dm   F

_ her. _____ Fe - ver. _____

Gtr. 7 (dist.)

𝆑

Gtr. 8 (dist.)

𝆑

Year in Review

Words and Music by Dan Auerbach, Patrick Carney and Brian Burton

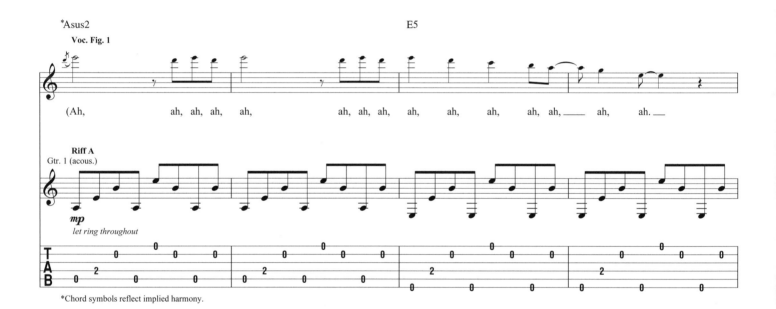

*Chord symbols reflect implied harmony.

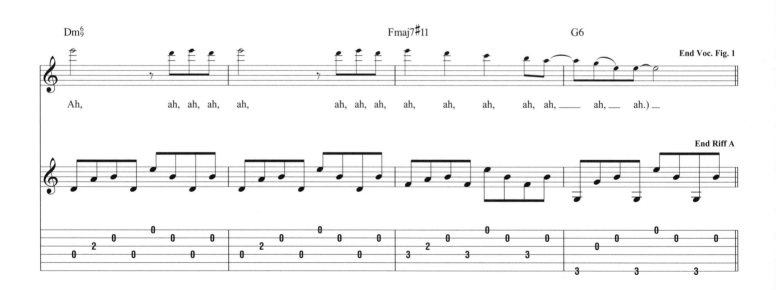

Copyright © 2014 McMoore McLesst Publishing (BMI) and Sweet Science (ASCAP)
All Rights on behalf of McMoore McLesst Publishing in the world excluding Australia and New Zealand Administered by Wixen Music Publishing, Inc.
All Rights on behalf of McMoore McLesst Publishing in Australia and New Zealand Administered by GaGa Music
All Rights Reserved   Used by Permission
- contains a sample from the song "Sandra" written by Nico Fidenco, publishing administered in the US and Canada by Sugar Melodi (ASCAP);
Administered ex. US and Canada by Una Societa del Gruppo Sugar.

such a shame. But you're do-in' it a-gain.
no sin. Will it ev-er end?

Chorus

Bkgd. Voc.: w/ Voc. Fig. 1
Gtr. 1: w/ Riff A

You don't want her no more. Ain't you been

down this road be-fore? So leave it a-lone,

Rhy. Fig. 1

To Coda ⊕

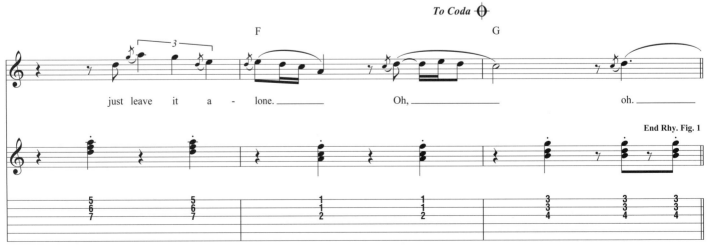

just leave it a-lone. Oh, oh.

End Rhy. Fig. 1

Interlude
Gtr. 2 tacet

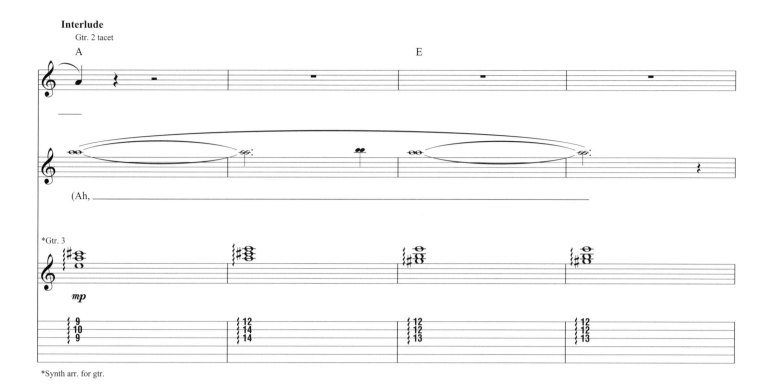

(Ah,

*Gtr. 3

mp

*Synth arr. for gtr.

D.S. al Coda

2. And when you

oo.)

Coda

Bkgd. Voc.: w/ Voc. Fig. 1
Gtr. 1: w/ Riff A

no, this __ ain't noth - in' __ new. The on - ly

thing   you've   got   is   you, _____   so   leave   it   a - lone, _____

just   leave   it   a - lone. _____   Oh, _____   oh. _____

Guitar Solo

Outro

Bkgd. Voc.: w/ Voc. Fig. 1
Gtr. 1: w/ Riff A (1st 4 meas.)

Gtrs. 4 & 5 tacet

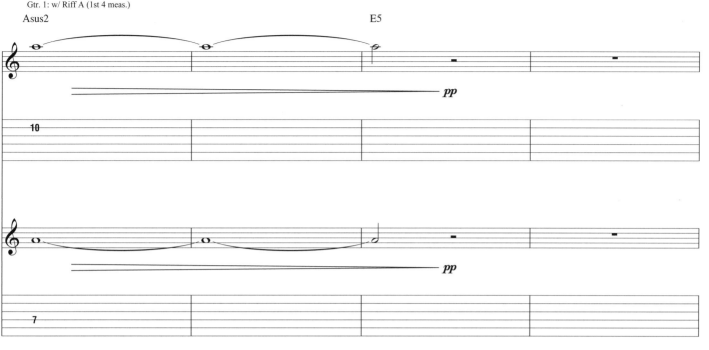

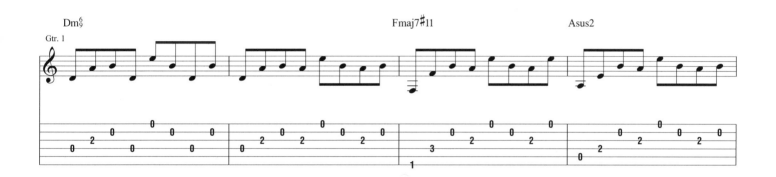

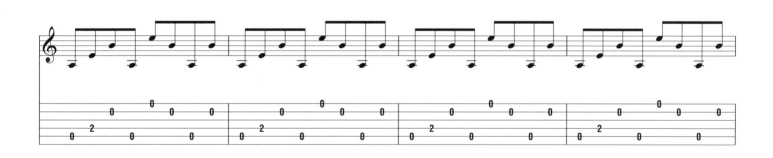

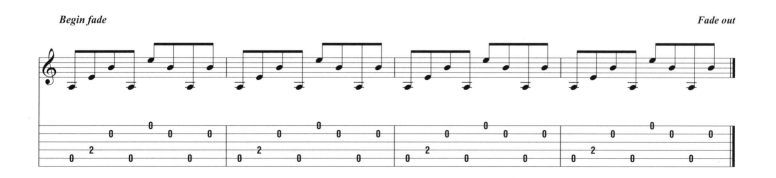

Bullet in the Brain

Words and Music by Dan Auerbach, Patrick Carney and Brian Burton

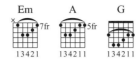

Intro
Moderately fast ♩ = 141
Half-time feel

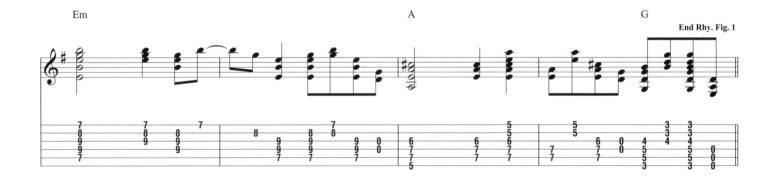

Chorus

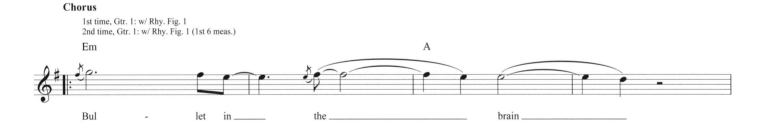

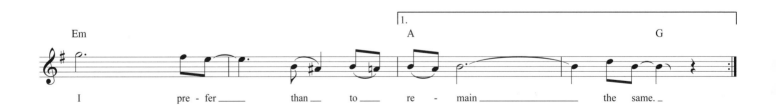

Copyright © 2014 McMoore McLesst Publishing (BMI) and Sweet Science (ASCAP)
All Rights on behalf of McMoore McLesst Publishing in the world excluding Australia and New Zealand Administered by Wixen Music Publishing, Inc.
All Rights on behalf of McMoore McLesst Publishing in Australia and New Zealand Administered by GaGa Music
All Rights Reserved   Used by Permission

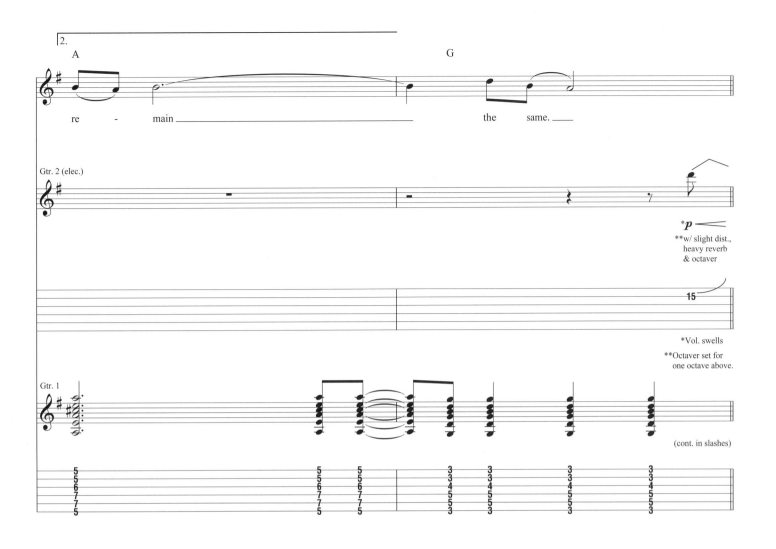

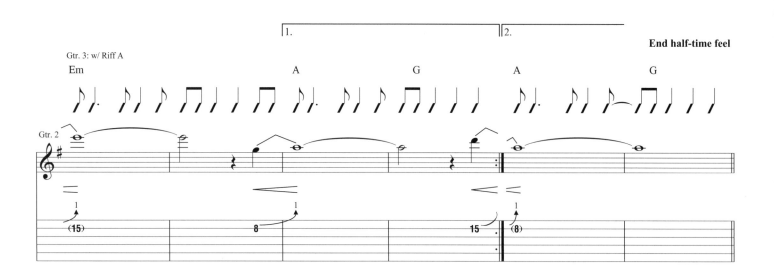

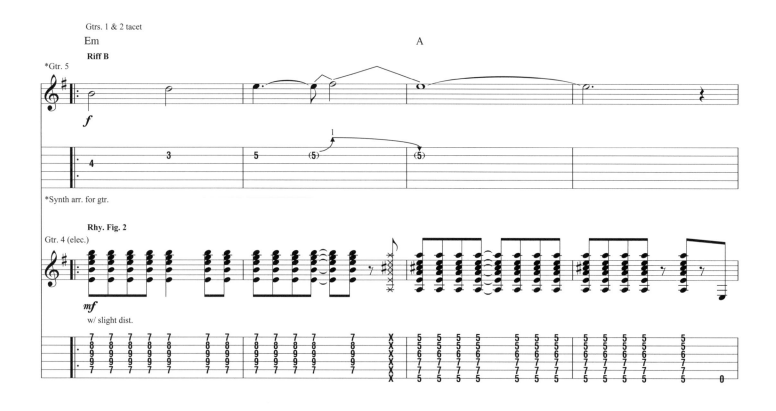

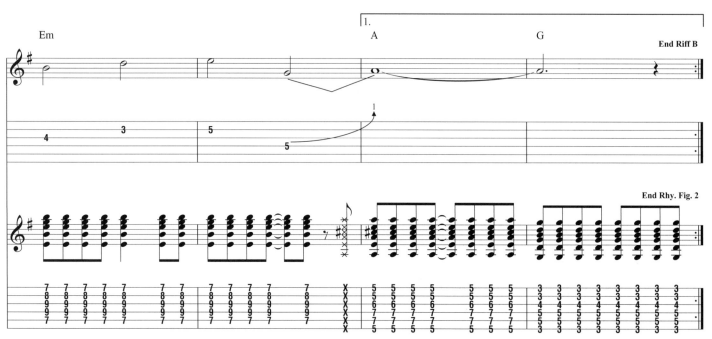

Fill 1
Gtr. 7

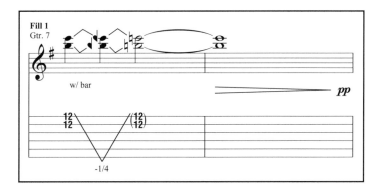

w/ bar

-1/4

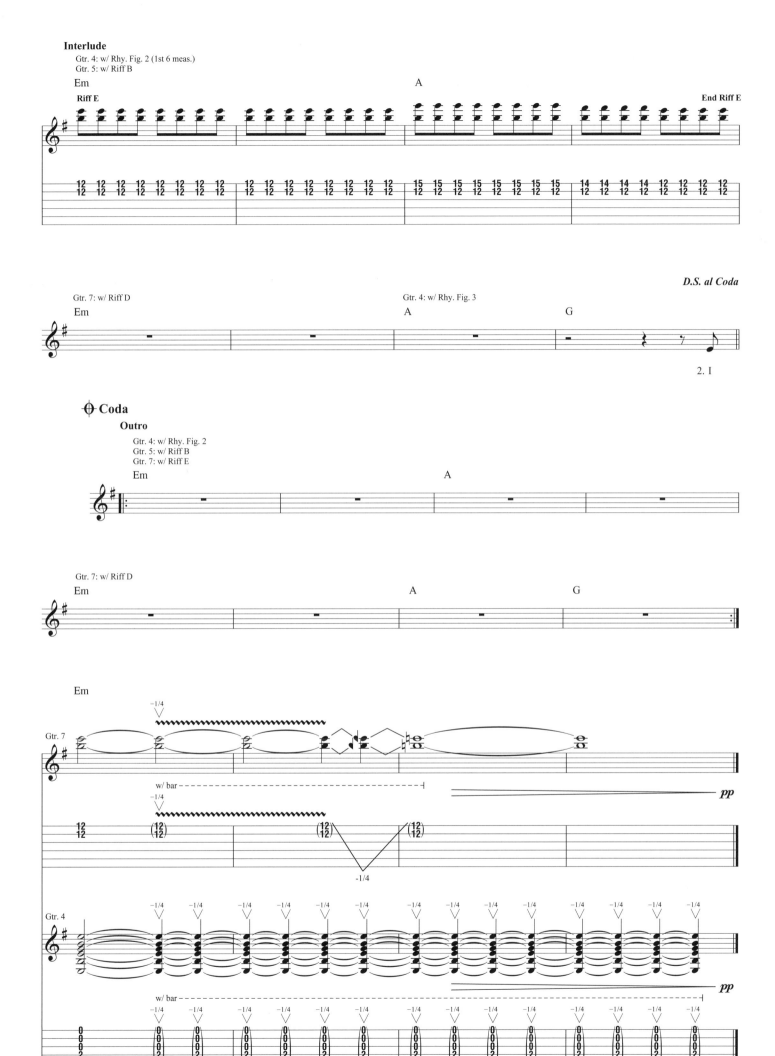

It's Up to You Now

Words and Music by Dan Auerbach and Patrick Carney

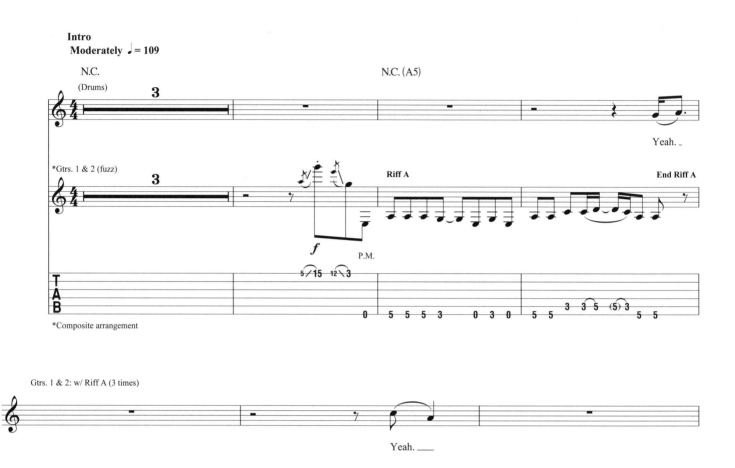

Copyright © 2014 McMoore McLesst Publishing (BMI)
All Rights in the world excluding Australia and New Zealand Administered by Wixen Music Publishing, Inc.
All Rights in Australia and New Zealand Administered by GaGa Music
All Rights Reserved   Used by Permission

Gtr. 2: w/ Riff A (4 times)

N.C. (A5)

Go to town.   It's   up   to   you

Riff C

Gtr. 1

P.M.   P.M.   P.M.   P.M.

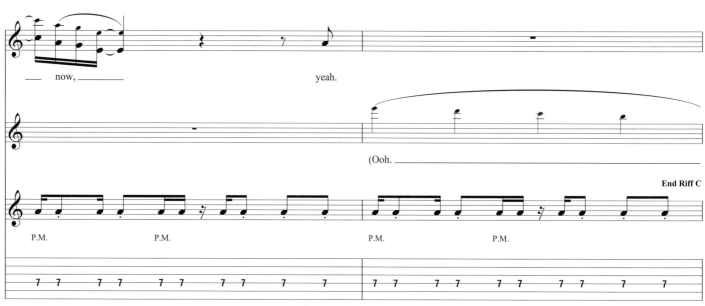

— now,   yeah.

(Ooh.

End Riff C

P.M.   P.M.   P.M.   P.M.

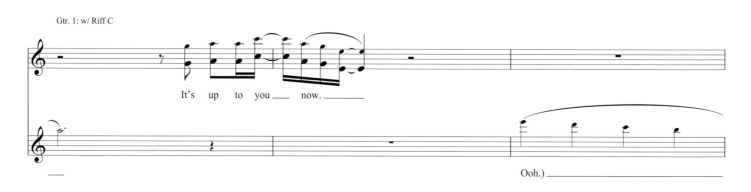

Gtr. 1: w/ Riff C

It's   up   to   you ___ now. ___

Ooh.)

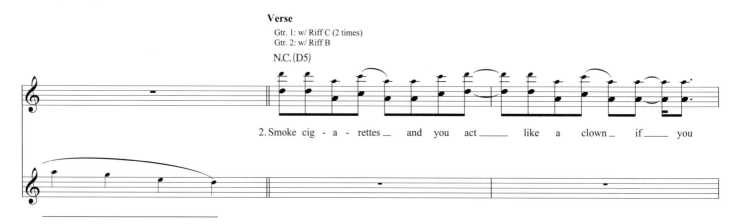

Verse

Gtr. 1: w/ Riff C (2 times)
Gtr. 2: w/ Riff B

N.C. (D5)

2. Smoke cig - a - rettes ___ and you act ___ like a clown ___ if ___ you

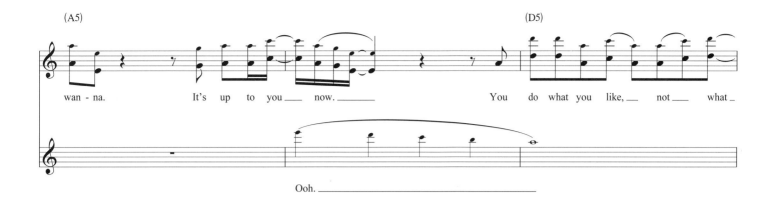

(A5)   (D5)

wan - na.   It's up to you __ now. _____   You do what you like, __ not __ what __

Ooh. _____

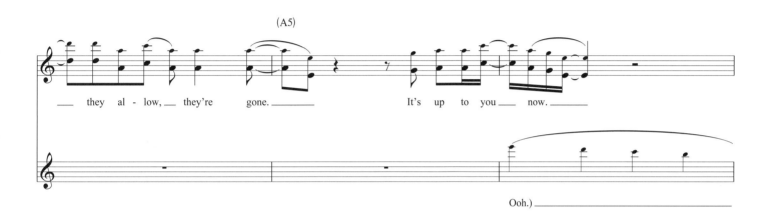

(A5)

__ they al - low, __ they're   gone. _____   It's up to you __ now. _____

Ooh.) _____

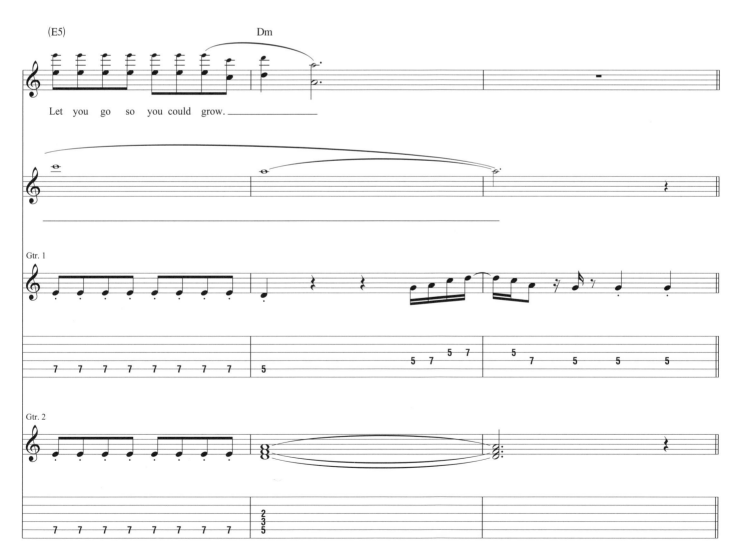

(E5)   Dm

Let you go so you could grow. _____

Gtr. 1

Gtr. 2

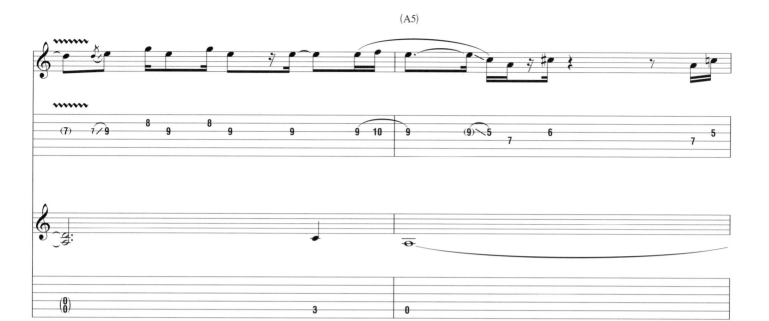

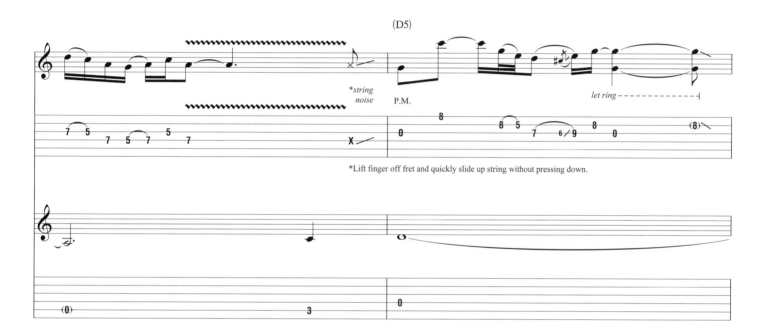

*Lift finger off fret and quickly slide up string without pressing down.

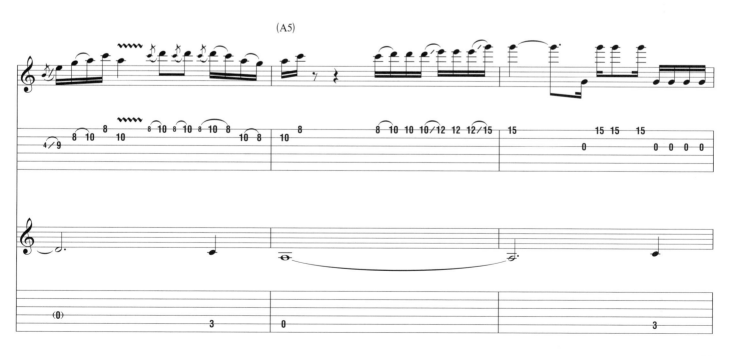

Outro
Tempo I

Gtr. 3 tacet

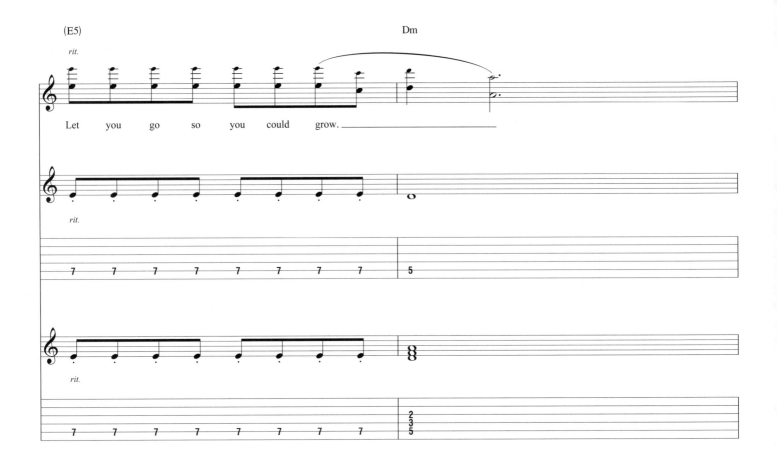

(E5)　　　　　　　　　　　　　　　　　　　Dm

rit.

Let you go so you could grow. _____

rit.

rit.

Free time

A5

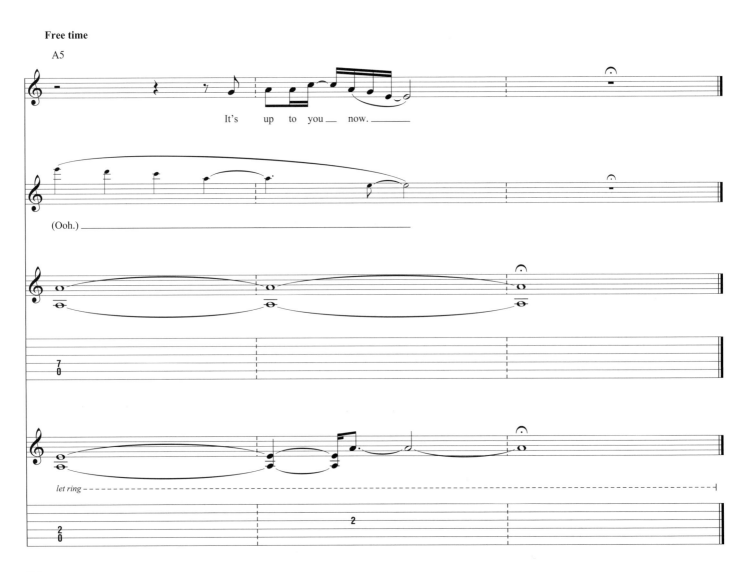

It's up to you ___ now. _____

(Ooh.) _____

let ring

Waiting on Words

Words and Music by Dan Auerbach, Patrick Carney and Brian Burton

Intro
Moderately slow ♩ = 76

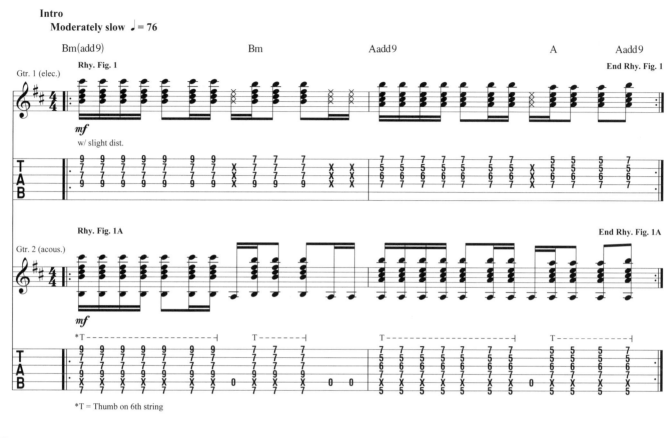

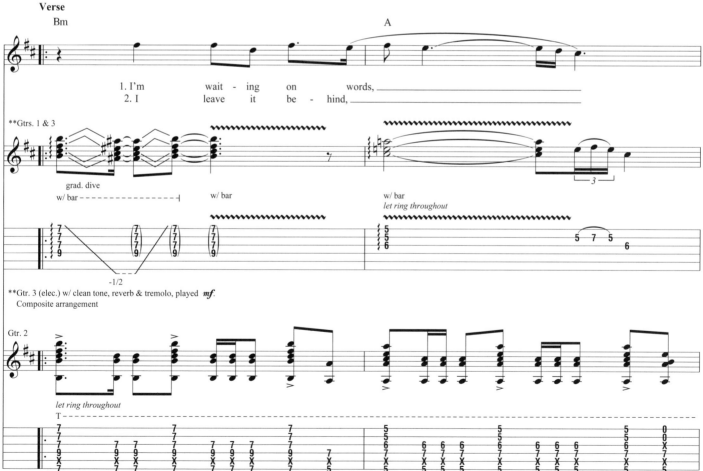

*T = Thumb on 6th string

**Gtr. 3 (elec.) w/ clean tone, reverb & tremolo, played *mf*.
Composite arrangement

Copyright © 2014 McMoore McLesst Publishing (BMI) and Sweet Science (ASCAP)
All Rights on behalf of McMoore McLesst Publishing in the world excluding Australia and New Zealand Administered by Wixen Music Publishing, Inc.
All Rights on behalf of McMoore McLesst Publishing in Australia and New Zealand Administered by GaGa Music
All Rights Reserved   Used by Permission

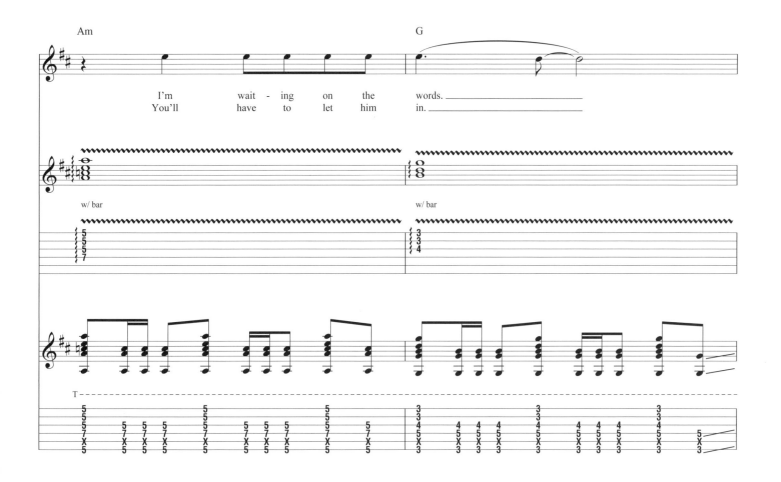

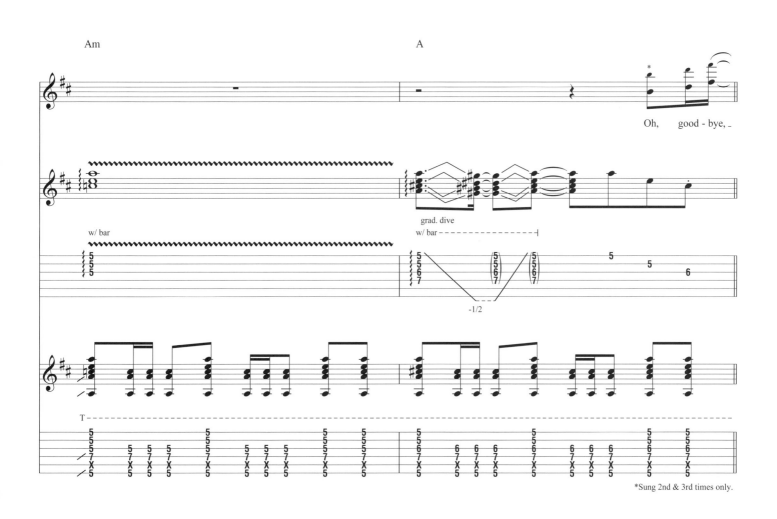

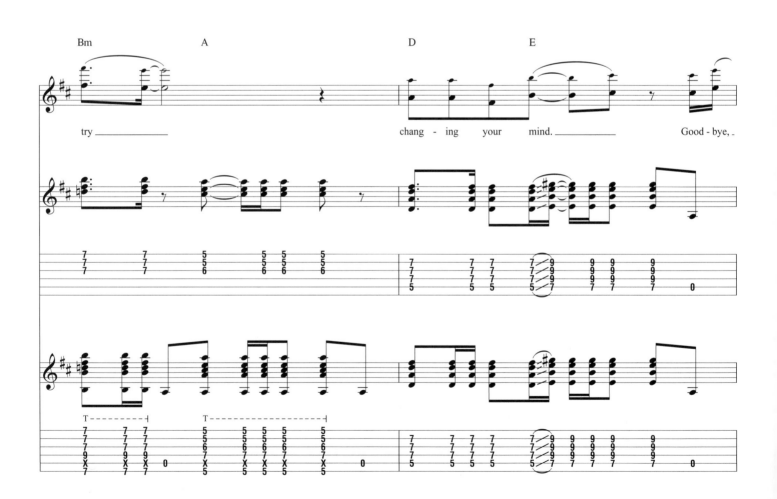

don't know where you're go - in'. The on -

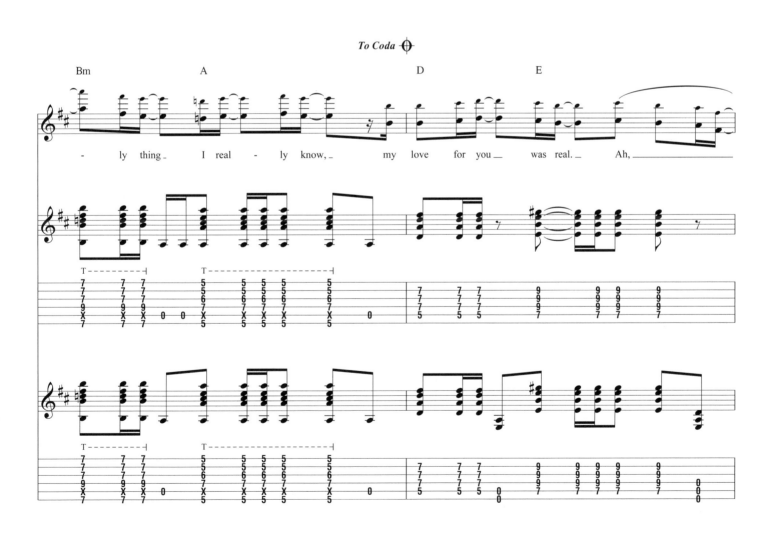

To Coda ✛

- ly thing __ I real - ly know, __ my love for you __ was real. Ah, __

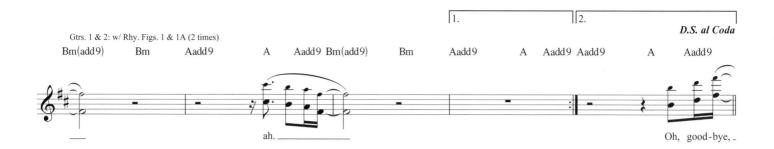

D.S. al Coda

Gtrs. 1 & 2: w/ Rhy. Figs. 1 & 1A (2 times)

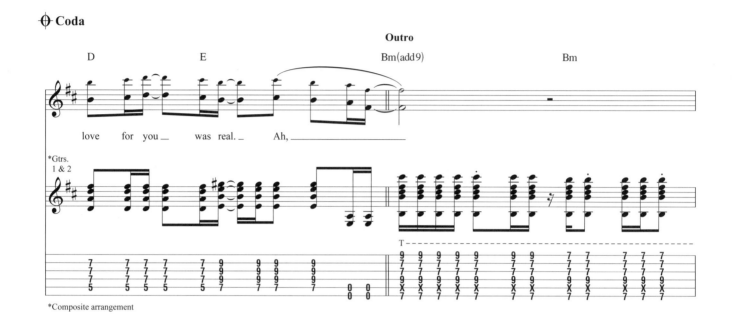

*Composite arrangement

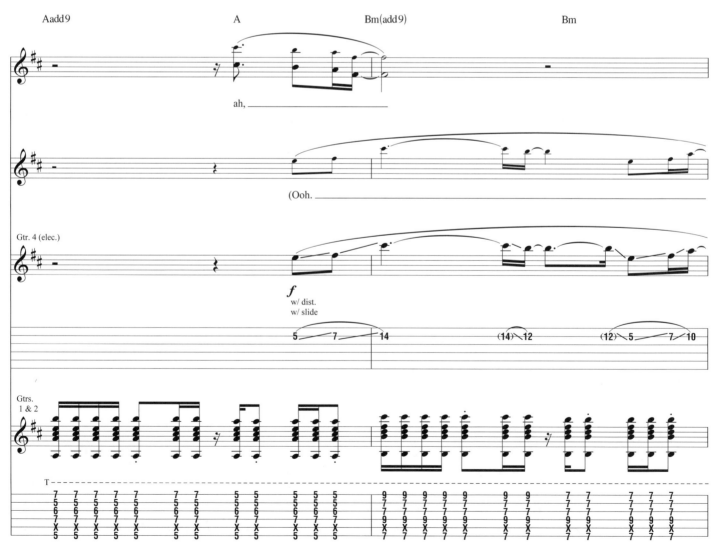

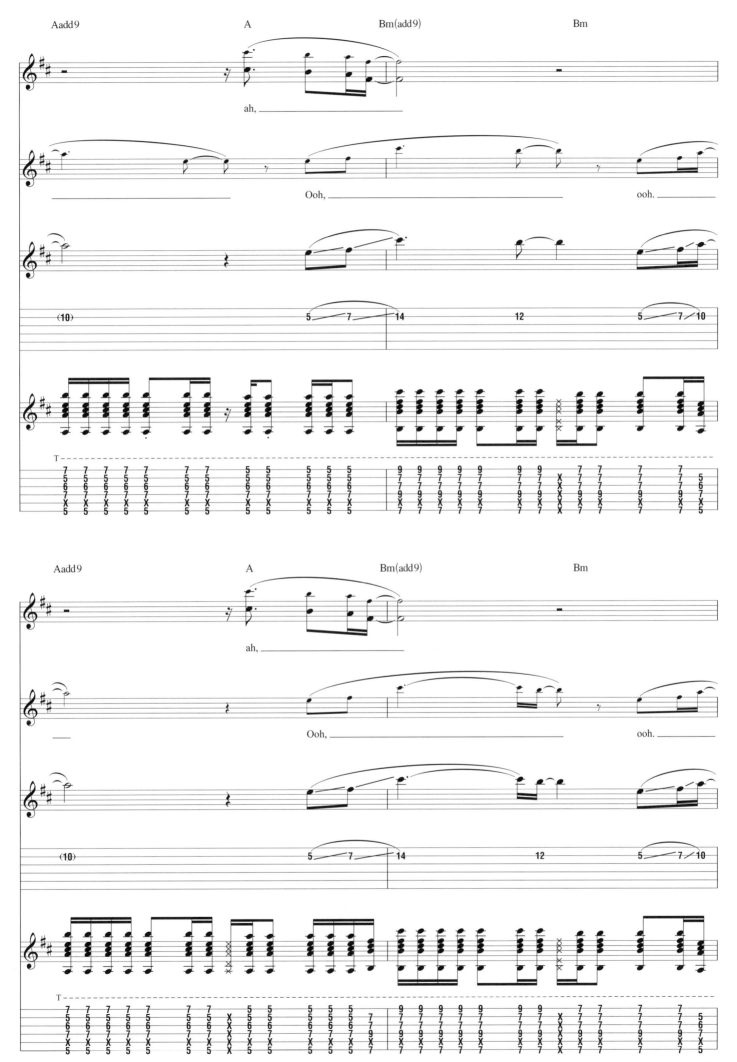

10 Lovers

Words and Music by Dan Auerbach, Patrick Carney and Brian Burton

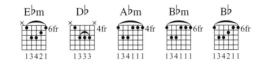

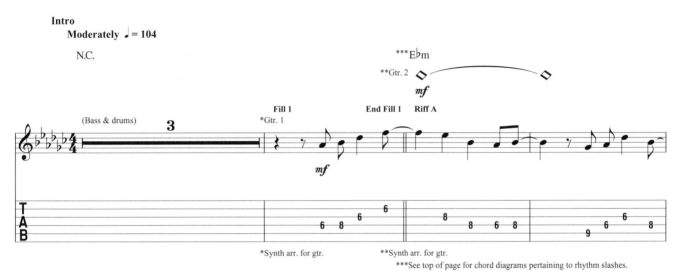

*Synth arr. for gtr.
**Synth arr. for gtr.
***See top of page for chord diagrams pertaining to rhythm slashes.

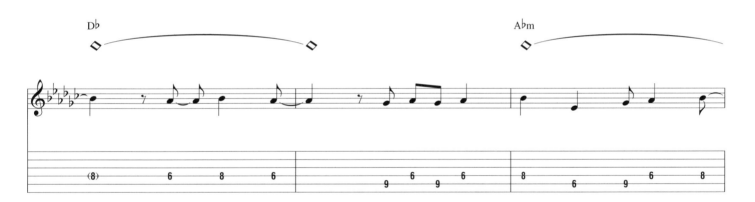

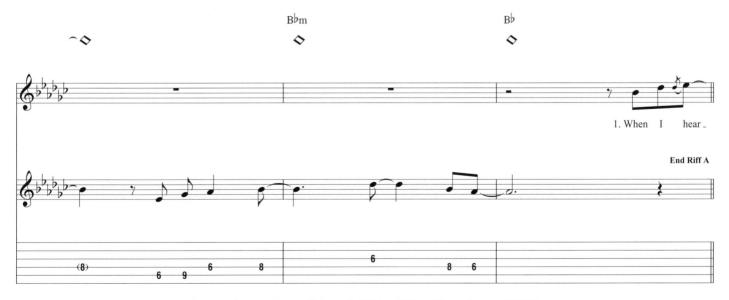

Copyright © 2014 McMoore McLesst Publishing (BMI) and Sweet Science (ASCAP)
All Rights on behalf of McMoore McLesst Publishing in the world excluding Australia and New Zealand Administered by Wixen Music Publishing, Inc.
All Rights on behalf of McMoore McLesst Publishing in Australia and New Zealand Administered by GaGa Music
All Rights Reserved   Used by Permission

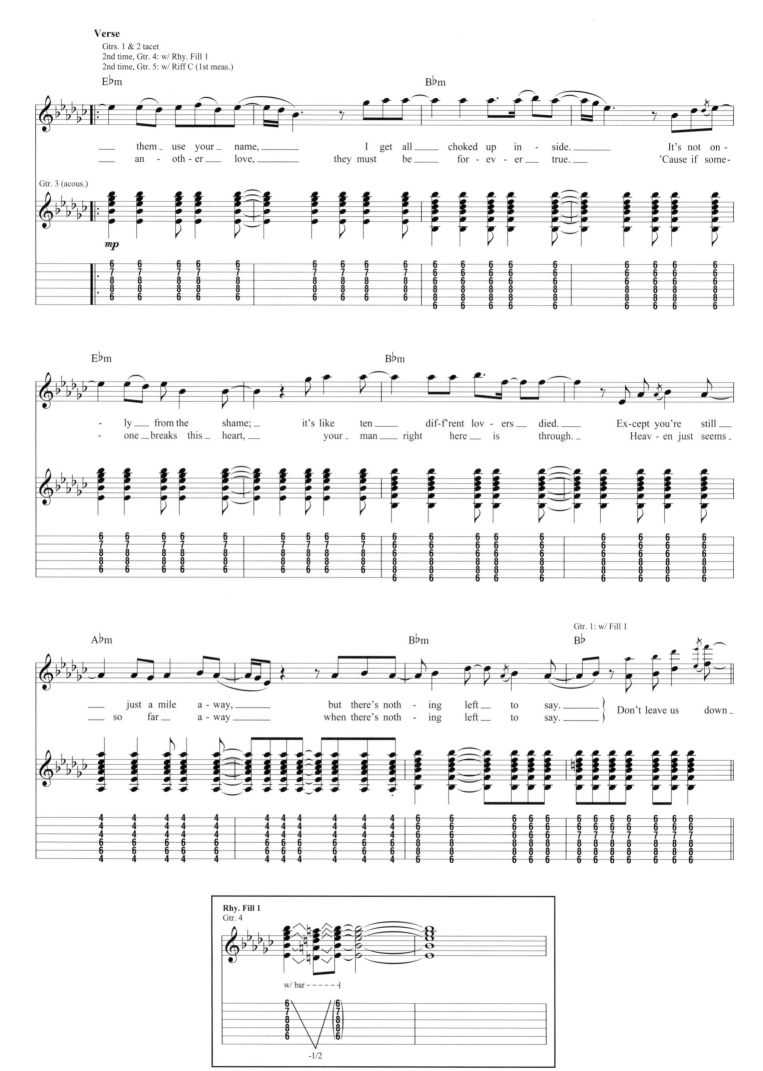

Chorus
1st & 2nd times, Gtr. 1: w/ Riff A
1st & 2nd times, Gtr. 3 tacet
3rd time, Gtr. 1: w/ Riff A (1st 7 meas.)
3rd time, Gtr. 6 tacet
E♭m
D♭
and out a - gain, 'cause we might break in - stead of bend.
Gtr. 5 (elec.)
Riff B
p
w/ slight dist.
Gtr. 4 (elec.)
Rhy. Fig. 1
mf
w/ clean tone
let ring
let ring
A♭m
I felt a lit - tle sting, then the pour - ing rain; it washed a - way

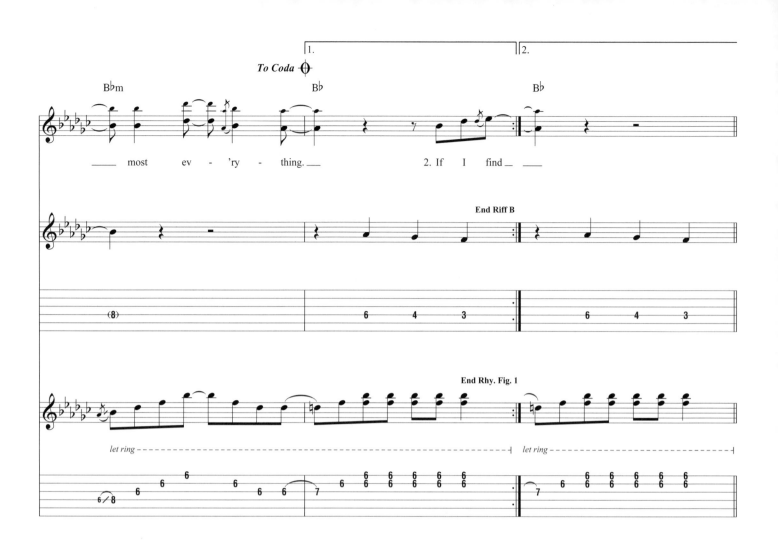

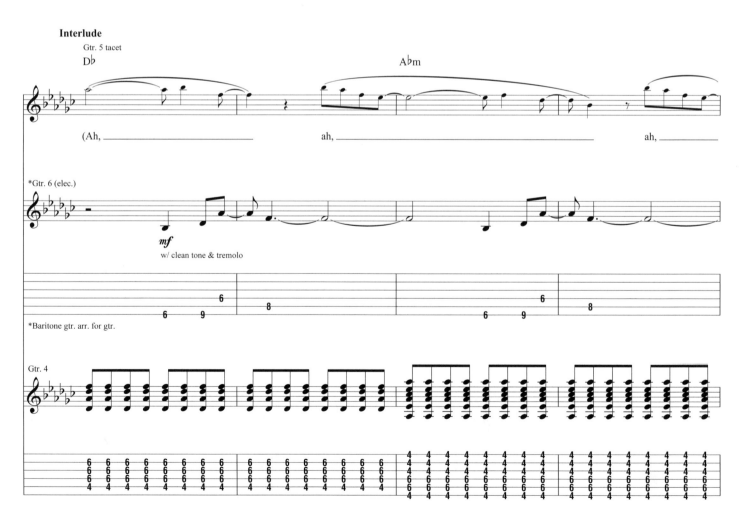

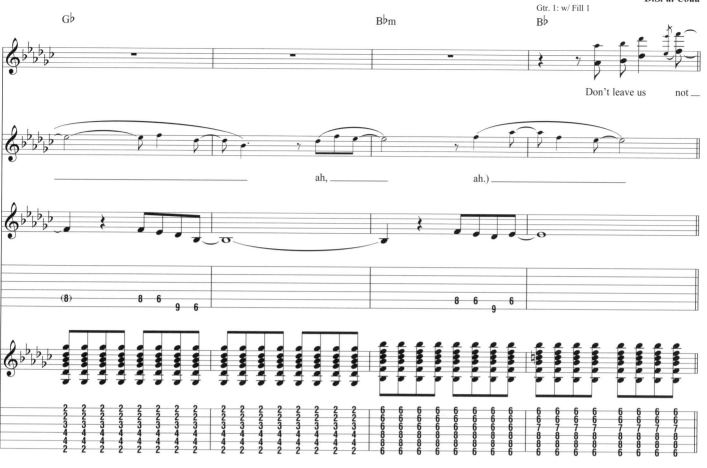

She's al - right, ___ but you're ___ all wrong. ___

Outro

Gtr. 1 tacet
Gtr. 4: w/ Rhy. Fig. 1
Gtr. 5: w/ Riff B

Gtr. 7 tacet

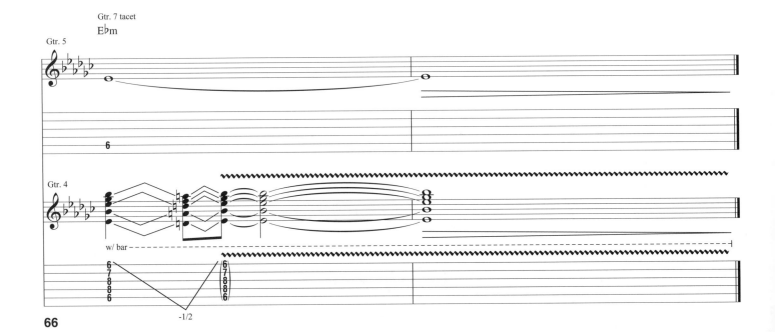

In Our Prime

Words and Music by Dan Auerbach, Patrick Carney and Brian Burton

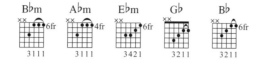

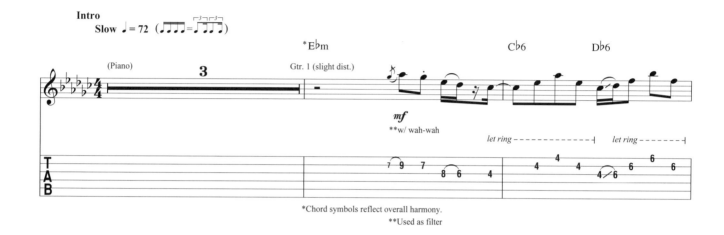

*Chord symbols reflect overall harmony.
**Used as filter

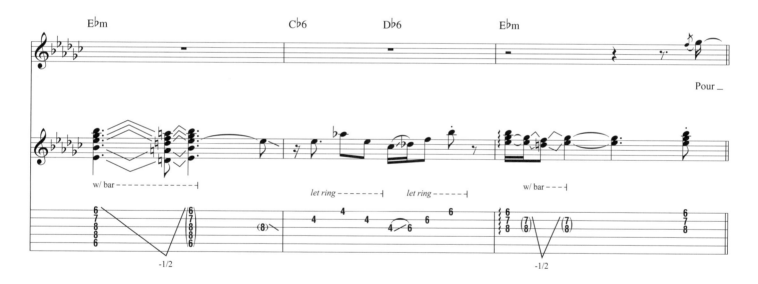

Copyright © 2014 McMoore McLesst Publishing (BMI) and Sweet Science (ASCAP)
All Rights on behalf of McMoore McLesst Publishing in the world excluding Australia and New Zealand Administered by Wixen Music Publishing, Inc.
All Rights on behalf of McMoore McLesst Publishing in Australia and New Zealand Administered by GaGa Music
All Rights Reserved   Used by Permission

it all ___ when we ___ were in ___ our prime. ___

Interlude
Faster ♩ = 84

Gtr. 1 tacet

Gtr. 3 (elec.)

*Gtr. 2

*Kybds. arr. for gtr.

Bridge

Rhy. Fig. 1A

Ev - 'ry now ___ and then ___ I see a face ___ from way back when and I ___ ex - plode. ___

Rhy. Fig. 1

My

O - pen my eyes.

w/ bar - - - - - -|

-1/2

Interlude

*Chord symbols reflect overall harmony.

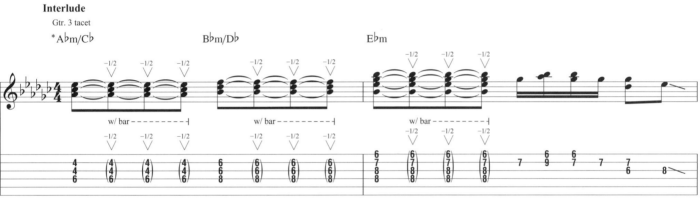

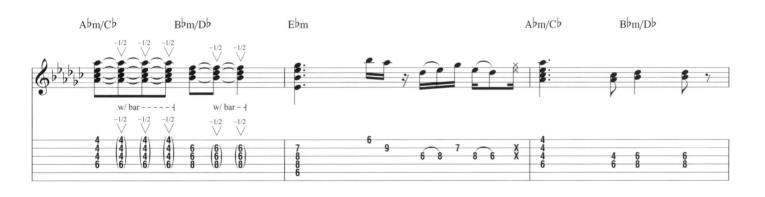

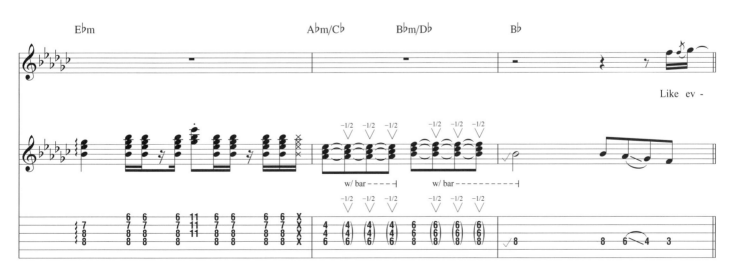

Like ev -

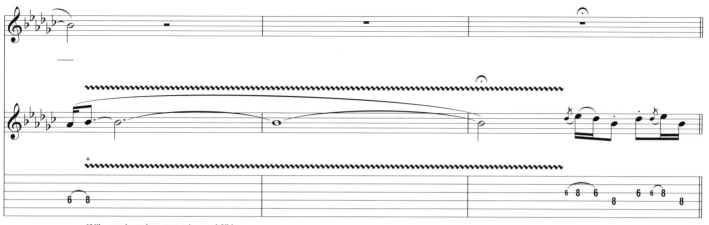

*Vib. sounds random open strings and fdbk.

Outro-Guitar Solo
A tempo

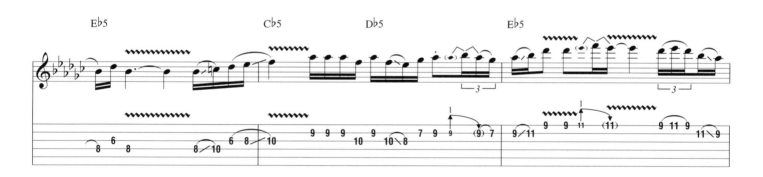

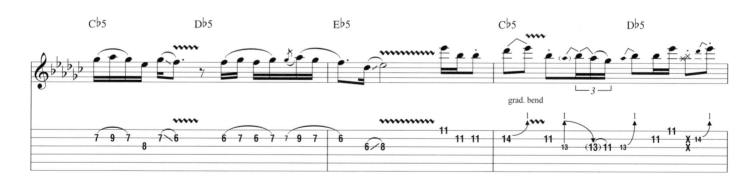

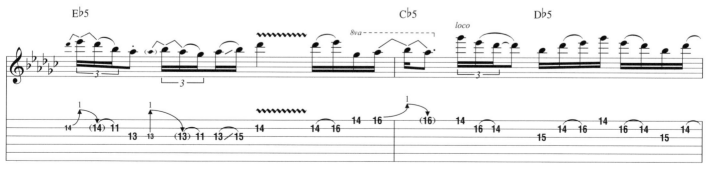

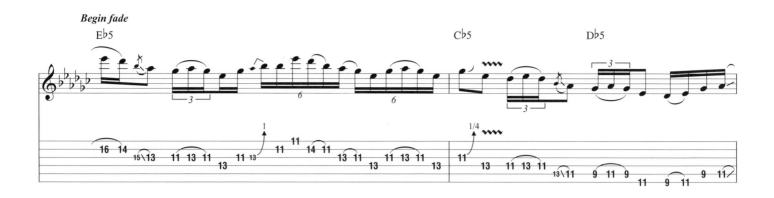

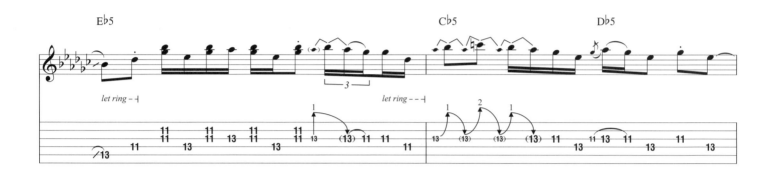

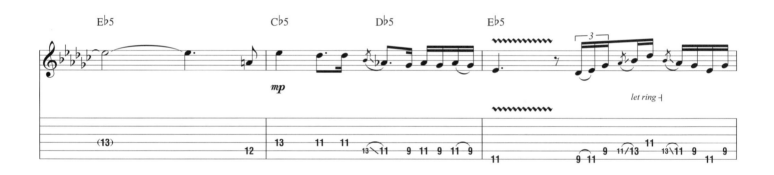

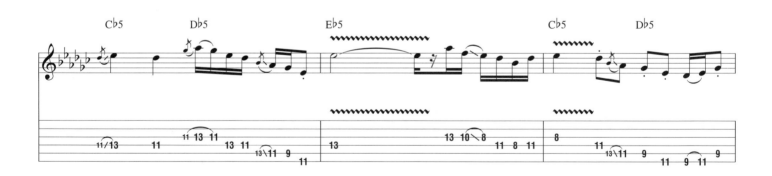

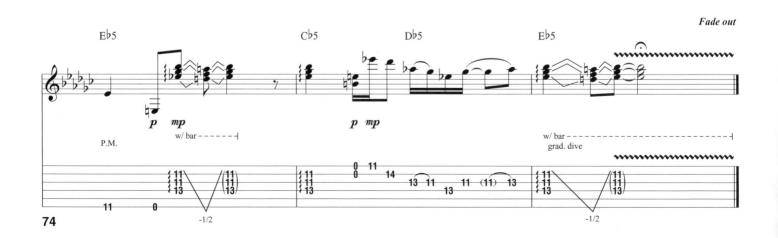

Gotta Get Away

Words and Music by Dan Auerbach and Patrick Carney

Gtrs. 1 & 2: Capo II

Gtr. 3: Open E tuning:
(low to high) E-B-E-G♯-B-E

Intro
Moderately fast ♩ = 132

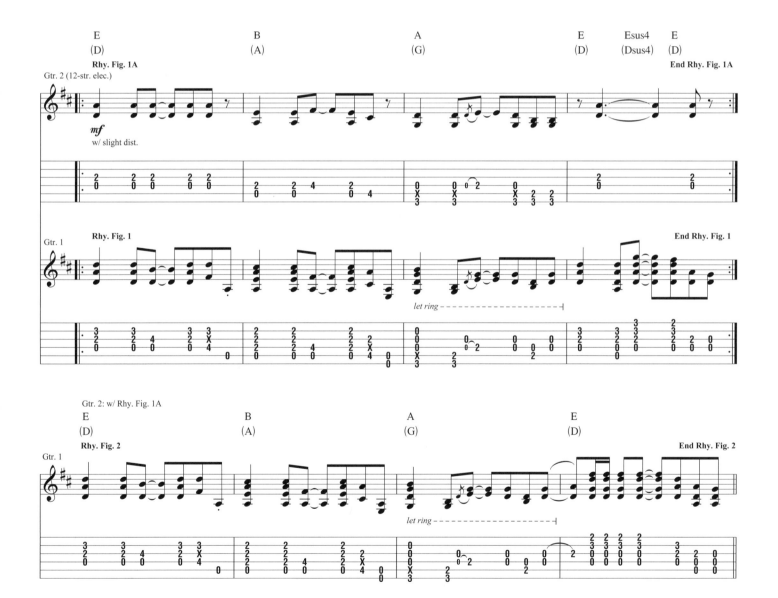

*Symbols in parentheses represent chord names respective to capoed guitar. Symbols above reflect actual sounding chord.
Capoed fret is "0" in tab. Chord symbols reflect basic harmony.

Copyright © 2014 McMoore McLesst Publishing (BMI)
All Rights in the world excluding Australia and New Zealand Administered by Wixen Music Publishing, Inc.
All Rights in Australia and New Zealand Administered by GaGa Music
All Rights Reserved   Used by Permission

3rd time, Gtr. 3 tacet

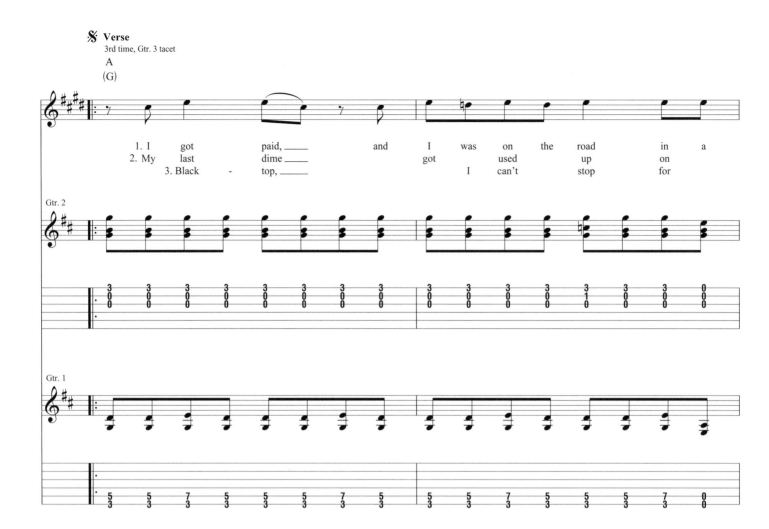

1. I got paid, _____ and I was on the road in a
2. My last dime _____ got used up on
3. Black - top, _____ I can't stop for

Gtr. 2

Gtr. 1

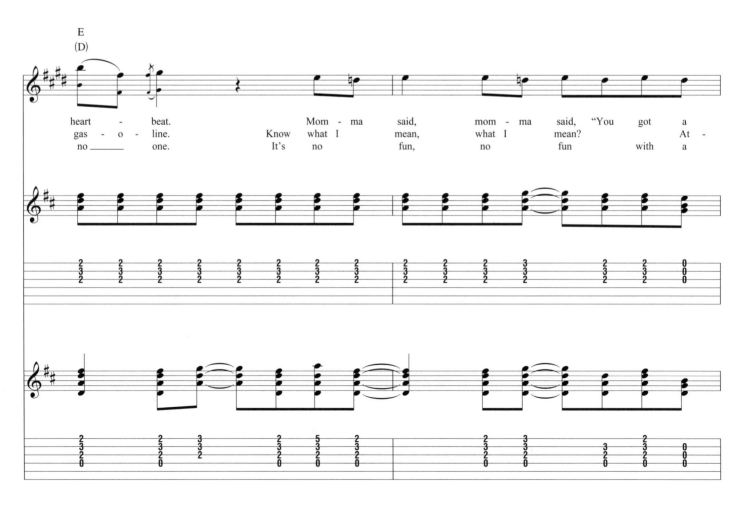

heart - beat. Mom - ma said, mom - ma said, "You got a
gas - o - line. Know what I mean, what I mean? At -
no _____ one. It's no fun, no fun with a

Chorus

1st & 2nd times, Gtr. 1: w/ Rhy. Fig. 1
3rd time, Gtr. 1: w/ Rhy. Fig. 1 (2 times)
Gtr. 2: w/ Rhy. Fig. 1A (2 times)

San Ber - doo _____ to Kal - a - ma - zoo _____ just _____

1st & 2nd times, Gtr. 1: w/ Rhy. Fig. 2

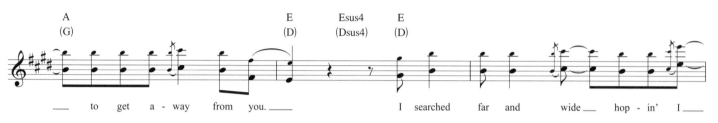

_____ to get a - way from you. _____ I searched far and wide _____ hop - in' I

To Coda ⊕

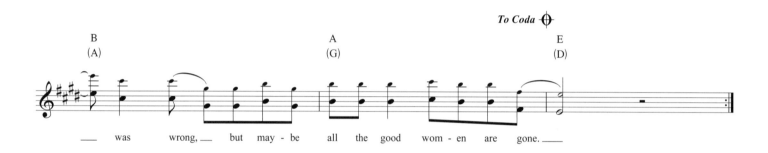

_____ was wrong, _____ but may - be all the good wom - en are gone. _____

Bridge

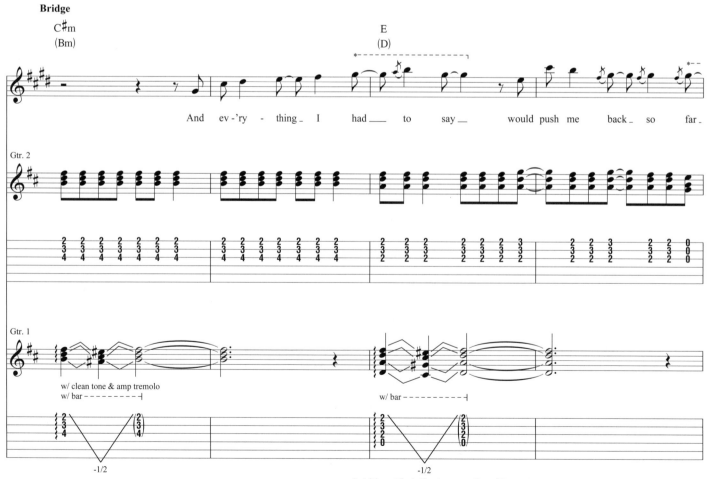

And ev - 'ry - thing _ I had _____ to say _____ would push me back _ so far _

w/ clean tone & amp tremolo
w/ bar - - - - - - - - ⌐

-1/2   -1/2

*w/ delay set for half-note regeneration w/ 2 repeats.

⊕ Coda

Chorus

Gtr. 1: w/ Rhy. Fig. 1 (1 3/4 times)
Gtr. 2: w/ Rhy. Fig. 1A (1 3/4 times)

I went from San Ber - doo __ to Kal - a - ma - zoo __ just __ to get a - way from you. __

I searched far and wide __ hop - in' I __ was wrong, __ but may - be all the good wom - en are

Free time

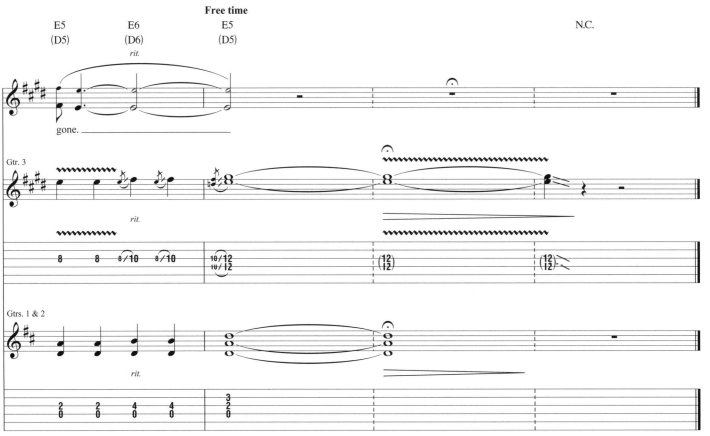

gone. _____